How full is your cup?

64 stories that can transform the way you look at life

D1513752

J M Sampath

INSIGHT
PUBLISHERS
nurturing wisdom

First edition published in 2010 by
Insight Publishers
17, I Cross, Gavipuram Extension
Bangalore - 560 019, Karnataka, India

ISBN 978-93-80738-01-7

© 2010 Insight Publishers

Printed at Pragati Offset Pvt. Ltd.
Hyderabad, India

Cover and illustrations by S. Muralidharan

Note from the Author

I present through the pages of this book, insights and wisdom, sought by our ancestors and passed on from one generation to the other through parables, stories and anecdotes. These are in essence, nothing but life's effort to preserve itself.

With the deepest sense of gratitude, I have collected some of these pearls of wisdom from the ocean of life and strung them for you to play with. I don't own these parables or stories as they belong to the spirit of human existence but it has been my humble attempt, through this book, to open up a significant perspective of life hidden between these wise lines and words. There are several other perspectives you can draw from these parables based on your own location in life and each of them can be a value-add to your own understanding of life. I hope every understanding that you extract from the following pages will enhance your capacity to draw more out of every context you come across and enrich the quality of life itself.

Just a word of caution: When we read a parable or story, there is a general tendency in each of us to slot people around us, who resemble the characters in the story and form conclusions about them. I request you to refrain from doing so, as this could restrict you from learning and growing, the way you otherwise can. It is a natural instinct in us to find faults, but what is more important is to use this instinct to continuously locate the faults in our own selves and rectify them. This will enable us to become what we are truly capable of being, rather than what we want to be. Incidentally there is a huge difference between the two.

Last but not the least, one of the important competencies that will be demanded of you in this era of consciousness, is your ability to reflect and stay with your thoughts to draw the most of it. This book is designed to nurture reflection in a way that can make you delve deeper into life and celebrate the very spirit of human existence!

Wishing you happy reading and insightful reflections!

J M Sampath

Foreword

A parable is a short story, a fictional narrative of events that might actually occur in nature. Usually the setting is recognisable and in the narrative there are very few details. The story is simple and the events are familiar. It is therefore easy for a listener or reader to understand and follow the very concrete account.

Yet a parable is hardly a simple story. A parable has surprising qualities. It is usually a metaphor. It carries a meaning that is beyond the actual word. The meaning often comes to us as a powerful moral or general principle of truth. From this surprising parable we learn something that can enrich our life in some or the other meaningful way.

So here is the trick. From the very concrete and simple parable, we often learn abstract and complex moral lessons. From the simple tool of the story-teller, we gain the precious gift of enlightenment.

Dr J. M. Sampath is a man with a deep understanding of life's most complex lessons. One of the most important things he understands is how to facilitate and effectively bring light to the mind of others. The subtitle of this book, '64 stories that can transform the way you look at life', is exactly what Dr. Sampath seeks to do. Using the simplest of parables and stories, he seeks to transform how you think, feel and see.

As you read the parables in this book, light will come to your mind and you will see differently. As this happens you are likely to desire to share the same light with others. As you use the parables in this book you will become like the author. You will help others transform how they look at life. You will be an effective facilitator with the transformational power to empower lives, just like you would have empowered your own!

Robert E. Quinn

(Author of 'Deep Change')

Well-respected author and thinker, Robert E. Quinn is a visionary authority on business leadership, organizational change and executive development. Author of several best-selling works like 'Deep Change' and 'Lift', Professor Quinn believes that people can create great change in large organizations by changing themselves. He also teaches at the Ross School of Business, Michigan and is known for his innovative instructional efforts.

*Dedicated to every
student of life...*

How full is your cup? 64 stories that can transform the way you look at life

 1
Eat your own fruit

 2
The miracle stone

 3
Destiny in a tossed coin

 4
Build wisely

 5
Growing

 6
How full is your cup?

 7
The cracked pot

 8
The filthy neighbour

 9
Who am I?

 10
I stopped long ago

 11
Present moment

 12
Change

 13
Cod liver oil for the dog

 14
All for the good

 15
Winning

 16
The lost key

 17
Mahan

 18
Fault finding

 19
This too shall pass

 20
Black balloon

 21
The holy cat

 22
The wooden bowl

 23
The royal pigeon

 24
Heart of a mouse

 25
Seeing

 26
A bowl of rice

 27
The golden eagle

 28
Human flaw

 29
Perfect man

 30
In the name of concern

 31
Bullseye

 32
The black book

 33

 33

33

The golden Buddha

 34

Compassion

 35

A tomb for Mr.Turtle

 36

Dream visitors

 37

Johnny complains

 38

Muddy road

 39

Wisdom

 40

After I am gone

 41

Set mind

 42

The poisonous arrow

 43

Convictions

 44

Meet me halfway

 45

Being appropriate

 46

Every minutes counts

 47

The transformation

 48

What I don't take is not mine

 49

Caring

 50

Chinese bamboo

 51

It's in your hands

 52

The sculptor

 53

Cut the rope

 54

The new robe

 55

How much land does a man need?

 56

Who is watching?

 57

Dandelions

 58

What next?

 59

The crossroads

 60

The one I feed

 61

Starfish

 62

The little girl who came with an umbrella

 63

Salt doll

 64

One step at a time

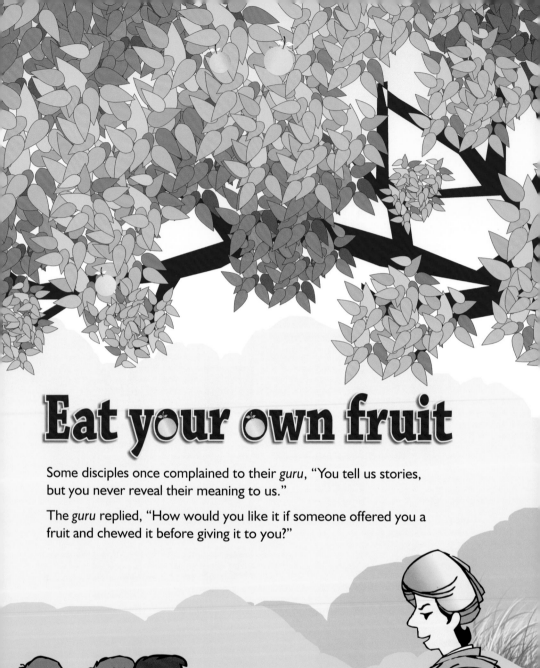

Eat your own fruit

Some disciples once complained to their *guru*, "You tell us stories, but you never reveal their meaning to us."

The *guru* replied, "How would you like it if someone offered you a fruit and chewed it before giving it to you?"

HOW DO YOU LEARN TO DRAW YOUR OWN INTERPRETATIONS OF LIFE THAN LIVE BY OTHERS' INTERPRETATIONS?

WHAT HOLDS YOU FROM THINKING BEYOND WHAT HAS BEEN THOUGHT?

THE MIRACLE STONE

A man once read in an ancient book about a black stone on the shores of the Black Sea, which could on contact, turn any metal into gold. The stone would be warm to the touch. So he went to the Black Sea and there, found a heap of black stones. He was convinced one of these would be the miracle stone.

He picked up a stone, felt it on his cheek, found it cold, and flung it into the sea. The second stone too was cold and followed the first one into the sea. He did this from morning to evening, every day for weeks, months and then years. Three years passed.

One day he put a stone to his cheek, threw it into the sea and then realized that was the stone he was looking for!

HOW EASILY DO
YOU GET USED TO WHAT
YOU ARE DOING?

WHAT HOLDS YOU FROM NOT
GETTING CONDITIONED?

HOW MANY OPPORTUNITIES
DO YOU MISS BECAUSE OF
YOUR OWN CONDITIONING?

Destiny
IN A TOSSED COIN

The Japanese General Nabunaga decided to attack even though he had only one soldier to the enemy's ten. He was sure he would win but his soldiers were full of fear.

On the way to the battlefield they stopped at a *Shinto* shrine. Nabunaga said to his army, "I shall now toss a coin. If it is heads, we shall win. If tails, we lose. Destiny will now reveal itself." He tossed the coin. It was heads.

The soldiers were so keyed up for the fight that they wiped out the enemy. Next day an aide said to Nabunaga, "No one can change destiny."

"Right," replied the General, showing him a coin that had heads on both sides.

HOW MUCH
DO YOU BELIEVE IN
YOURSELF?

WHO DECIDES YOUR
DESTINY?

Build Wisely!

There lived an elderly carpenter. One day he thought to himself...

It is time I retired and enjoyed a life of leisure...

When the employer learnt of his wish to retire, he was indeed sorry to let go of one of his best workers. However, he said,

Build just one last house for me, this will entirely be your baby. Consider it a personal favour!

The carpenter reluctantly agreed. But it was easy to see that his heart was not in his work.

He resorted to shoddy workmanship and used inferior material, thereby saving some money for himself.

When the house was ready, the employer came to inspect it...

The very next day, a grand farewell was arranged in the new house and handing over the door key to the carpenter, the employer proudly declared...

This is your home! A token of appreciation for your dedicated service.

The carpenter was shocked!

What a shame! Had he only known he was building his own house!

DO YOU HAVE MULTIPLE STANDARDS...ONE FOR YOURSELF AND ANOTHER FOR OTHERS?

WHAT STOPS YOU FROM GIVING YOUR BEST TO EVERYTHING YOU DO?

GROWING...

A museum, well-known for its marble sculptures, attracted large admiring crowds. A brilliantly sculpted statue of a lady was one of the masterpieces that adorned the resplendent hall.

One night, the marble tile, on which the lady stood, complained, "It is not fair! We both originated from the same cave and yet people walk over me and admire you for hours. Why am I a stepping stone and you a masterpiece?"

The marble lady replied calmly, "Remember the day the sculptor tried to work on you with his chisel and the fuss you created, discouraging him to work any further? But when he chose me instead, I allowed him to complete what he had started. It was painful no doubt, but even you would agree that the end result was worth it!"

From then on the marble tile took pride in being a stepping stone and never complained again.

5

HOW STRONG IS YOUR
RESISTANCE TO LIFE'S EFFORT
IN SHAPING YOU?

DO YOU ALLOW LIFE TO
SCULPT YOU TO BECOME
WHAT YOU ARE
ACTUALLY CAPABLE OF BEING?

IF NOT, WHY NOT?

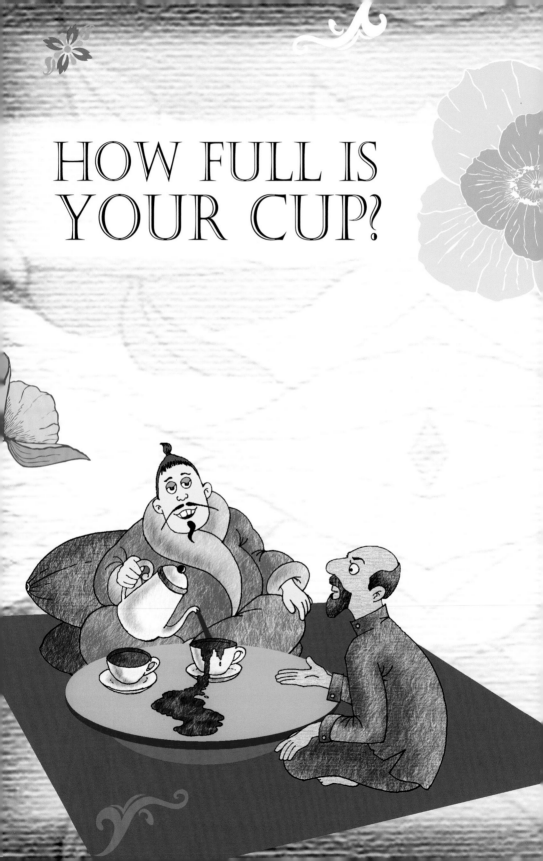

HOW FULL IS YOUR CUP?

A *Zen* master received a university professor who came to enquire about *Zen*.

The master served tea, filling his visitor's cup to the brim, and continued pouring.

The professor watched him until he could no longer restrain himself. "It is full. No more will go in!"

"Like this cup," the master said, "you are full of your own opinions and speculations. How can I show you *Zen* unless you first empty your cup?"

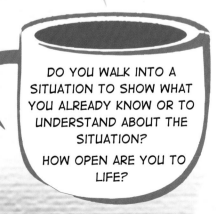

DO YOU WALK INTO A SITUATION TO SHOW WHAT YOU ALREADY KNOW OR TO UNDERSTAND ABOUT THE SITUATION?

HOW OPEN ARE YOU TO LIFE?

The cracked pot

A water bearer carried two pots, slung from the ends of a pole. One was a whole pot and other had a crack.

The whole pot was proud of its perfection and the other, ashamed of its deformity. One day, the cracked pot pleaded, "Master, why do you continue to use me when I can deliver only half my load?"

Understanding the pot's dilemma, the water bearer said, "Look on the sides of the path we take everyday." The pot did and was pleasantly surprised to see a bed of vibrant flowers on its side, whereas the other side was dry and barren! "You may not be delivering your full load, but you are the reason for these lovely flowers, which I take to my master for his daily prayers!" concluded the wise man.

THE FILTHY NEIGHBOUR

...the streaks are on your window!

HOW OFTEN DO YOU CLEAN YOUR GLASSES BEFORE YOU SEE OTHERS?

HOW OBJECTIVE ARE THE GLASSES YOU WEAR?

Who am I ?

The Wemmicks were small wooden people, carved by a woodworker named Eli. Every Wemmick looked different. But they did the same thing all day. They gave each other stickers. The talented and pretty ones always got stars. But the Wemmicks with rough surfaces and chipped paint got dots, which meant they were no good.

Punchinello always got dots even though he tried hard to earn stars. Soon he started believing he was a no-good Wemmick. One day he met a Wemmick called Lulia with no dots or stars. It wasn't that other Wemmicks didn't try to give her stickers; it was just that the stickers did not stick on her. Punchinello was curious to know how this was possible and Lulia asked him to meet Eli.

Punchinello felt very happy in Eli's company. "Don't worry about your dots," Eli said. "After all, they are given by fellow Wemmicks. But you are special to me because I made you."

"But why don't stickers stick on Lulia," he asked. "Because the stickers only stick if you let them!" Punchinello thought "I think Eli really means it." And at that moment a dot fell to the ground. Soon he had no stickers sticking to him and he felt good deep within.

9

HOW MUCH DO YOU
GET CARRIED AWAY
BY WHAT OTHERS
THINK OF YOU?

WHAT HOLDS YOU
FROM ACCEPTING
YOURSELF AS YOU
ARE DEEP WITHIN?

I STOPPED LONG AGO...

A woman was at her singing lessons. She had such a jarring voice that her neighbour could take it no more. He managed to finally summon up the courage to knock at her door and say, "Madam, if you don't stop your singing, I think I'll go mad!"

"What are you talking about?" said the woman. "I stopped two hours ago!"

10

DO YOU RESPOND TO
PEOPLE OR THE IMAGE
YOU HOLD OF THEM?

WHY DO YOU IMPRISON
PEOPLE IN YOUR MIND?

WHAT PREOCCUPATIONS
OF YOURS PREVENT
YOU FROM SEEING LIFE
AS IT IS?

Once the clock master, while fixing a clock heard the pendulum plead, "Please sir, leave me alone. Think of the number of times I will have to tick day and night, sixty times each minute, sixty minutes an hour, twenty four hours a day, three sixty five days a year, for year upon year... I could never do it."

But the master replied wisely, "Don't think of the future. Just do one tick at a time and you will enjoy every tick for the rest of your life." And the pendulum decided to follow the master's words and is still ticking away merrily.

AS YOU ARE PULLED BY THE PAST AND THE FUTURE, HOW MUCH OF THE PRESENT DO YOU MISS OUT?

WHAT DOES IT TAKE TO BE IN THE PRESENT?

Change...

The *Sufi* Bayazid says this about himself- I was a revolutionary when I was young and my only prayer to God was...

"Lord, give me the energy to change the world."

As I approached middle age and realised that half my life was gone without my changing a single soul, I changed my prayer to...

"Lord, give me the grace to change all those who come in contact with me. Just my family and friends and I shall be content."

12

But now that I am old, I pray thus...

"Lord, give me the grace to change myself. If I had prayed for this right from the start I would not have wasted my life."

WHAT MOTIVATES YOU TO ATTEMPT CHANGING OTHERS?

WHAT HOLDS YOU FROM SEEING YOURSELF AS THE BEGINNING OF ALL CHANGE YOU WANT TO SEE IN THE WORLD?

COD LIVER OIL FOR THE DOG

A man began to give large doses of cod liver oil to his pet dog because he had been told that it was good for dogs. Each day he would hold the protesting dog between his knees, force its jaws open and pour the oil down its throat.

One day the dog broke away and spilt the oil on the floor. Then to the man's great surprise, it not only lapped up the oil that was spilt on the floor but came back to lick the spoon.

That was when the man discovered that, what the dog had been fighting was not the oil but the manner in which it was being given.

WHAT IS MORE
IMPORTANT...'GIVING' OR
'GIVING YOUR WAY'?

HOW CAN YOU BECOME
SENSITIVE TO OTHERS'
WAY OF RECEIVING?

All for the Good

A close aide of the king had the habit of looking at every situation, good or bad, and commenting, "All for the good". This habit landed him in trouble one day when on a hunting trip, due to a faultily loaded gun, the king's finger was blown off. The aide remarked, "All for the good". The king was furious at such insensitiveness and had him imprisoned.

A few months later, while on a hunt, the king was captured by some cannibals, who had the custom of sacrificing a human to their deity. As they were preparing to sacrifice the king, they noticed the king's missing finger and being too superstitious to sacrifice a less than perfect specimen to their deity, set him free.

The king realised the truth behind the comment and summoned his aide. He narrated his near brush with death and apologised for his hasty decision. True to form, the aide remarked, "All for the good." The king was surprised, but the aide explained, "Had your majesty not imprisoned me, I would have surely accompanied you on the hunt and the cannibals would have had no problem sacrificing a 'perfect' specimen like me to their deity."

The king, amused by his aide's attitude, rewarded him and made him his chief advisor.

DO YOU SEE LIFE FILLED WITH INDEPENDENT EVENTS OR A SERIES OF EVENTS, IN TURN CONNECTED WITH A BIGGER PURPOSE?

WHEN WILL YOU START SEEING LIFE AS A WHOLE?

Winning

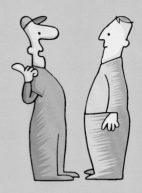

15

A farmer whose corn always took the first prize at the State Fair, had the habit of sharing his best corn seeds with all the farmers in the neighbourhood. When asked why, he said, "It is really a matter of self-interest. The wind picks up the pollen and carries it from field to field, so if my neighbours grow inferior corn, the cross pollination brings down the quality of my own corn. So I am concerned that they plant only the very best."

WHAT DOES IT MEAN TO WIN WITH EVERYONE INVOLVED BEING HAPPY?

WHAT DOES IT TAKE TO GIVE AND STILL NOT LOSE?

HOW SURE ARE YOU OF YOUR OWN SELF?

THE LOST KEY

A neighbour found Nasruddin on his hands and knees near a lamp post, searching for something. The neighbour asked, "What are you searching for?"

"My key."

Now, both men got on their knees to search. After a while the neighbour asked, "Where did you lose it?"

"At home."

"Good Lord! Then why are you searching here?"

"Because it is bright here!"

16

DO YOU END UP
SEARCHING FOR SOLUTIONS
WHERE IT IS CONVENIENT,
RATHER THAN WHERE YOU
ACTUALLY NEED TO
LOOK FOR THEM?

HOW SERIOUS ARE YOU
ABOUT SOLVING YOUR
PROBLEMS?

MAHAN

Along the bottom of the river Ganges lived a village of creatures whose way of life was to cling tightly to the rocks on the river bed, and to resist the current of the river. One of them, 'Siddharth the adventurous', got tired of clinging. The monotony wearied him. He decided to place his trust in the current and allow it to take him where it would. His parents and friends cautioned him about the current, "It will smash you against the rocks and kill you." But Siddharth did not heed them and let go. Immediately he stumbled and was tossed against the hard rocks, which strengthened Siddharth's resolve not to cling again.

17

In time, the current lifted him free from the bottom and he got bruised and hurt no more. The clinging creatures saw him and marvelled at him, hailing him as 'Mahan - the Great'. Siddharth swaying in the current said, "I am no greater than any one of you. Dare to let go and the river will lift you free and you will discover your true worth." The creatures, still clinging, cried, "Mahan!" Siddharth flowed past, leaving the creatures to cling and make legends of a Mahan.

WHAT ARE SOME OF THE THINGS YOU ARE CLINGING TO?

WHAT HOLDS YOU FROM LETTING GO?

FAULT FINDING

The pupils of the Tendai school used to study meditation before *Zen* entered Japan. Four of them, who were very close friends, promised one another to observe seven days of silence.

On the first day all were silent. Their meditation had begun auspiciously, but when night fell and the oil lamps were growing dim, one of the pupils could not help exclaiming to a servant, "Fix those lamps!"

The second pupil was surprised to hear the first one talk. "We are not supposed to say a word," he remarked.

"You two are stupid. Why did you talk?" asked the third.

"I am the only one who has not talked," announced the fourth pupil.

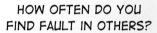

HOW OFTEN DO YOU FIND FAULT IN OTHERS?

WHAT HOLDS YOU FROM USING THIS INSTINCT TO FIND AND RECTIFY SOME OF YOUR OWN FAULTS?

THIS TOO SHALL PASS

Once upon a time there lived a king who was very powerful. His court was attended by wise men from many lands. One day he gathered them and announced, "I wish to test your wisdom. Bring for me, before sunset, a gift that will make me joyous when I am unhappy and sober when I am indulgent."

In the evening he called for the wise men to see what they had brought for him. The wise men paid their respects to the king and placed before him a ring on which was inscribed, "This too shall pass."

THIS TOO SHALL PASS

HOW STUCK ARE YOU WITH THE PLEASURES AND PAINS OF LIFE?

IS THERE ANYTHING THAT IS PERMANENT?

HOW DO YOU KEEP MOVING FORWARD IN LIFE?

Black Balloon

Raju was a dark complexioned little boy. He stood watching the balloon man at the country fair attracting customers by releasing a red balloon, a blue balloon, a yellow one and a white one. They all went soaring into the sky until they disappeared. The little boy asked, "Sir, if you send the black one up would it go as high as the others?"

The balloon man, understanding the boy's question, snapped the string that held the black balloon and as it soared upwards said,

"It is not the colour son. It's what is inside that makes it rise."

20

WHAT MAKES
YOU FEEL INFERIOR
OR SUPERIOR TO
OTHERS?

ARE YOU NOT
UNIQUE AND MUCH
MORE THAN HOW
YOU LOOK AND
WHAT YOU HAVE?

The holy cat

Each time the *guru* sat for worship with his
disciples, the *ashram* cat would come and
distract them. So he ordered them to tie her
up when the *ashram* was at prayer. After the
guru died, the cat continued to be tied up at
worship time. When the cat expired, another cat
was brought into the *ashram* to make sure that
the *guru*'s orders were observed faithfully at
worship time.

Centuries passed and learned treatises
were written by the *guru*'s scholarly
disciples on the ritualistic
significance of tying up a cat
while worshipping.

21

WHAT HOLDS YOU
FROM SEEKING TO
KNOW WHY YOU DO
WHAT YOU DO?

HAVE YOU BOTHERED
TO UNDERSTAND THE
PURPOSE BEHIND MANY
OF THE THINGS YOU
DO IN LIFE?

The wooden bowl

A frail old man went to live with his son, daughter-in-law, and a four-year old grandson. The old man's hands trembled, his eyesight was blurred, and his step faltered. The family ate together every night at the dinner table. But the old man's shaky hands and failing sight made eating rather difficult. Peas rolled off his spoon and when he grasped the glass, milk often spilled on the table cloth.

The mess irked the son and his wife. "We must do something about father," said the son. I've had enough of his spilled milk, noisy eating and food on the floor. So a small table was set in the corner, where grandfather was to eat alone while the rest of the family enjoyed dinner at the table. Since grandfather had broken a dish or two, his food was served in a wooden bowl. Often when the family glanced in grandfather's direction, he had a tear in his eye as he ate alone. The four-year-old watched it all in silence.

22

One evening the father noticed his son playing with wood scraps. He asked the child, "What are you making son?" The boy looked up from his project and sweetly replied, "Oh, I am making a little bowl for you and mama to eat your food from when I grow up." The four-year-old smiled innocently and went back to work.

The parents were speechless. Then tears started to stream down their cheeks. Though no word was spoken, both knew what must be done. That evening the husband took grandfather's hand and gently led him back to the family table. For the remainder of his days he ate every meal with the family. And for some reason, neither husband nor wife seemed to care any longer when a fork was dropped, milk spilled or tablecloth soiled.

ARE YOU WORRIED THAT YOUR CHILDREN DON'T LISTEN TO YOU?

INSTEAD SHOULDN'T YOU BE MORE WORRIED THAT THEY ARE WATCHING YOU?

23

Nasruddin became the Prime Minister. Once when he was wandering through the palace gardens he saw a royal falcon. Nasruddin had never seen such a bird before, and thought it was an ill-kept pigeon. He ordered his men to catch it. When they brought it to him, Nasruddin took a pair of golden scissors and trimmed the claws, wings and beak of the falcon. "Now you look like a decent pigeon," he said. "Your keeper has evidently been neglecting you."

DO YOU ACCEPT PEOPLE AS THEY ARE OR KEEP TRIMMING THEM UNTIL THEY LOOK LIKE HOW YOU WANT THEM TO?

HOW CONSCIOUS ARE YOU OF YOUR INVISIBLE SCISSORS?

Heart of a mouse

According to an ancient Indian fable, a mouse was in constant distress because of its fear of the cat. A magician took pity on it and turned it into a cat. But then it became afraid of the dog. So the magician turned it into a panther whereupon it was full of fear of the hunter. At this point the magician gave up.

He turned it into a mouse again saying, "Nothing I do for you is going to be of any help because you have the heart of a mouse."

24

DO YOU REALISE THAT LASTING CHANGE IS POSSIBLE ONLY WHEN YOU WORK AT THE CAUSE LEVEL?

DO YOU FOCUS ON CAUSE OR THE MERE SYMPTOMS WHILE WORKING ON YOUR OWN LIMITATIONS?

seeing

There was an old blind woman who lived with her daughter in a little fishing village on the sea shore. The daughter dived for pearls, which she sold to the local agent and from the proceeds, they lived their lives. However, before selling each day's collection, the daughter kept aside in a little bag some of the choicest pearls as a hedge against difficult times.

One day, during a dive, the daughter was attacked by a shark and killed. The mother was desolate as not only had she lost her only child and companion but also her only means of support. In the midst of her grieving and loss she remembered the little bag of pearls that her daughter had kept aside and decided to sell them to the agent for her own livelihood.

25

The agent examined the pearls and paid her the exact market value for them and advised her about investing the money so that she would have a regular income for the rest of her life.

When the old woman had gone, the agent's assistant who had observed the whole deal asked, "Those were black pearls and you paid their full value! Why did you do that? After all, the woman was blind and could not see the colour of the pearls!" The agent replied,

"But I am not blind and I can see."

HOW OFTEN DO YOU SEE BEYOND WHAT IS VISIBLE?

WHAT STOPS YOU FROM SEEING THAT WHICH NEEDS TO BE SEEN?

HOW AWARE ARE YOU OF THE CONTEXT?

A bowl of rice

When *Buddha* was travelling from place to place, people gathered around him seeking advice. A young woman once came to him with great sorrow and pain in her heart. Her son had died and she could not contain her grief. She came to *Buddha* for solace. *Buddha* told her to go to the town and bring a bowl of rice from a home that had not seen sorrow.

She went from house to house saying "Can you give me a bowl of rice?"

"Yes", the woman of the house would say.

26

"But had there been any great sorrow in this home, I cannot accept your bowl of rice."

So she went from house to house but could not find a single home from which she could accept a bowl of rice. Soon she realised that birth and death were a part of existence and her sorrow vanished.

BLINDED BY EMOTIONS, DO YOU FAIL TO SEE THE UNIVERSALITY OF LIFE?

PLEASURE OF ARRIVAL AND PAIN OF DEPARTURE ARE TWO SIDES OF THE SAME COIN. CAN YOU AFFORD TO GET STUCK TO EITHER?

27

A man found an eagle's egg and placed it under a brooding hen. The eagle hatched with the rest of the chickens and grew to be like them. He clucked and cackled; scratched the earth for worms; flapped his wings and managed to fly a few feet in the air. Years passed. One day, the eagle, now a little older, saw a magnificent bird above him in the sky. It glided in graceful majesty against the powerful wind, with scarcely a movement of its golden wings. Spellbound, he asked...

"Who is that?"

"That's the king of the birds, the eagle. He belongs to the sky. We belong to earth, we're chickens."

So the eagle lived and died a chicken, for that's what he thought he was!

YOU ARE WHAT YOU BELIEVE YOU ARE.

WHAT HAVE YOU GROWN UP BELIEVING?

IS IT NOT TIME TO EXAMINE SOME OF YOUR BELIEFS?

HUMAN FLAW

There was once a scientist who discovered the science of reproducing himself so perfectly that it was impossible to tell the reproduction from the original.

One day he learnt that the Angel of Death was searching for him. So he reproduced a dozen copies of himself. The angel was at a loss to know which of the thirteen specimens before him was the scientist, so he left them all alone and returned to heaven.

28

But not for long, for being an expert in human nature, the angel came up with a clever plan. He said, "Sir, you must be a genius to have succeeded in making such perfect reproductions of yourself. However, I have discovered a flaw in your work, just one tiny little flaw."

The scientist immediately jumped out and shouted, "Impossible! Where is the flaw?" "Right here," said the angel, as he picked up the scientist from among the reproductions and carried him off.

IS YOUR PERFECTION JUST LIMITED TO WHAT YOU DO OR DOES IT TRANSCEND YOUR SKILLS AND EVOLVE YOU INTO A FINE HUMAN BEING?

WHAT ARE SOME OF YOUR FLAWS?

Perfect Man

I have heard about a man who remained a bachelor his whole life because he was in search of a perfect woman. When he was seventy, somebody asked, "You have been travelling and travelling – from New York to Kathmandu, from Kathmandu to Rome, from Rome to London, and you have been searching. Could you not find a perfect woman? Not even one?"

The old man became very sad. He said, "Yes, once I did. One day, long ago, I came across a perfect woman."

The inquirer asked, "Then what happened? Why didn't you get married?"

The old man replied sadly, "What to do? She was looking for the perfect man."

In the name of concern...

One day, a tiny opening appeared in a cocoon. A man sat and watched the butterfly for several hours as it struggled to force its body through the little hole. Then suddenly it seemed to stop making any progress. It appeared as though it had got as far as it could and could go no further.

The man, in earnest, took a pair of scissors and cut open the cocoon, to help the poor creature. He was glad to see the butterfly emerge easily. But it had a withered body and shrivelled wings. The man waited anxiously for the wings to open, expand and support the butterfly's body. Nothing happened! The tiny butterfly spent the rest of its life crawling around with a withered body and shrivelled wings. It never knew what it felt to fly.

What the man, in all his kindness and goodwill, did not understand was that the restricting cocoon that made the butterfly struggle to get through its tiny opening was nature's way of forcing fluid from the body of the butterfly into its wings, so that it would be ready for flight once it achieved its freedom from the cocoon.

HOW MUCH DO YOU UNDERSTAND WHAT IS GOOD FOR WHOM?

IS YOUR SUPPORT ENABLING OR DISABLING SOMEONE'S GROWTH?

BULLS EYE

A man saw many targets with a perfect bullseye on each one of them. "There must be an extremely talented shooter around," he thought in amazement. Just then he saw a boy with a set of bows and arrows in his hand. He asked him, "Have you shot these perfect targets?"

Pat came the reply "Yes! I shot them all!" Now the man was even more impressed. "How could you be so perfect every time?" he asked.

"It's so easy!" exclaimed the boy. Saying so he shot an arrow in the air, and promptly went and drew a bullseye around the spot where the arrow had landed!

The black book

One day a grieving man came to Hodja - the judge.

"Your cow has killed mine!" He cried.

Hodja shouted, "You silly man, how can the cow know that it is a crime to kill another cow. Case dismissed!"

"Pardon me," said the man. "I said it wrong. My cow has killed yours."

"Oh! Then that is another problem," said the judge. "Lets open the black book and see what it says."

HOW DIFFERENT ARE THE STANDARDS YOU HAVE SET FOR YOURSELF FROM THE ONES SET FOR OTHERS?

HAVE YOU STUDIED YOUR BLACK BOOK?

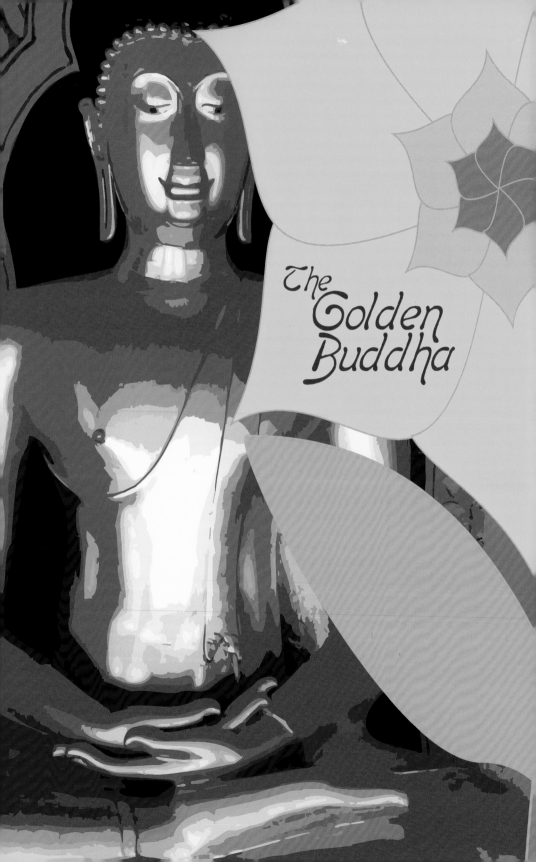

The Golden Buddha

33

Built during the
Sukhothai Period, the ten
feet high statue of the
seated *Buddha* was made
of pure gold and weighed
nearly six tons, one of the
finest of its kind in the world.
This enormous masterpiece
shone with such brilliance that
even the most jaded were awed
by its quiet overwhelming strength.

The story of the Golden *Buddha* is
intriguing because it had to be
camouflaged to protect its identity when
the Burmese were about to attack the
city. The statue was covered in plaster to
conceal it from the invaders' greedy eyes.
The camouflage job turned out to be so good
that when those who covered it died, so did the
secret of the treasure inside.

Two centuries after it had been first covered, the
statue when being moved to a new temple in Bangkok,
happened to slip from a crane and fell into the mud. According
to temple lore, a monk, who had dreamed that the statue was
divinely inspired, went to see the statue and through a crack in the
plaster, saw a glint of gold and soon discovered its true nature for the
world!

WHAT HAVE YOU
COVERED YOURSELF WITH?

ARE YOU WAITING FOR AN
ACCIDENT TO DISCOVER
WHAT YOU ARE ACTUALLY
MADE UP OF?

Compassion

34

Every morning when the Prophet passed by an old woman's house, she would empty a basket of rubbish on his head from the upper storey of her house. He never once remonstrated with her about this. One day, when the Prophet passed by the house, no rubbish fell on his head.

Thinking the old woman must be ailing, he went upstairs to inquire and found her ill in bed. When she discovered that the Prophet had come to meet her, she began to weep, "I ill-treated you all these years and now you come to inquire after my health!"

Ultimately she became one of his true followers.

WHAT IS THE EXTENT OF YOUR TOLERANCE?

WILL IT BE POSSIBLE FOR YOU TO CARE FOR THOSE WHO HURT YOU?

WHAT ARE THE PRECONDITIONS YOU PLACE ON YOUR RELATIONSHIPS?

A tomb for Mr. Turtle

A little boy was heartbroken to find his pet turtle lying on its back, lifeless and still, beside the pond. His father did his best to console him, "Don't cry, son. We'll arrange a lovely funeral for Mr. Turtle. We'll make him a little coffin all lined in silk and get the undertaker to make a headstone for his grave, with Mr. Turtle's name carved on it. Then we'll have fresh flowers placed on the grave each day and make a little picket fence to go all around it."

The little boy dried his eyes and became enthusiastic about the project. When all was ready, a cortege was formed - father, mother and child, who began to move solemnly towards the pond to bring in the body.

35

But the body had vanished! Suddenly they spied Mr. Turtle emerging from the depths of the pond merrily. The little boy stared at his father in bitter disappointment and cried out...

"Let's kill him!"

WHAT ALL HAVE YOU KILLED THUS FAR WITH YOUR OBSESSION?
WHAT WOULD IT TAKE TO KILL YOUR OBSESSION?

Dream Visitors

"Our schoolmaster used to take a nap every afternoon," related a disciple of Soyen Shaku. We children asked him why he did so and he would say, "I go to dreamland to meet the old sages, just as Confucius did." It seems when Confucius slept, he would dream of ancient sages and later tell his followers about them.

It was extremely hot one afternoon and some of us took a nap. Our schoolmaster scolded us and demanded an explanation. "We went to dreamland to meet the ancient sages, just as Confucius did," we explained. "And what was the message from those sages?" the schoolmaster demanded. "We met the sages and asked them if our schoolmaster came there every afternoon," one of us replied, 'but they said that they had never seen any such fellow!"

36

JOHNNY COMPLAINS...

Johnny made friends with a goat named Billy. He would give some grass and lettuce as breakfast to Billy and spend hours in his company everyday.

One day Johnny, hoping a change of diet would do his new friend a lot of good, offered him rhubarb instead of grass. Billy nibbled a bit but decided he didn't want it and pushed it away. Johnny caught Billy by one of his horns and forced him to eat the rhubarb. The goat butted Johnny gently at first and when resistance increased, Johnny stumbled and fell on his back. Johnny was so offended that he walked away never to return.

37

Some days later, when his friend asked him why
he never went to play with Billy, he replied.....

**"Because he
rejected me!"**

WHEN OTHERS FAIL
TO ACCEPT WHAT YOU
GIVE THEM, WHY DO
YOU FEEL REJECTED?

WHEN YOU GIVE
SOMETHING OUT OF
YOUR OWN FREEDOM,
DO YOU ALLOW OTHERS
TO ALSO EXERCISE THEIR
FREEDOM TO ACCEPT
THE SAME OR NOT?

MUDDY ROAD

Tanzan and Ekido were once travelling together down a muddy road. A heavy rain was falling. Coming around a bend, they saw a lovely girl in a silk kimono and sash, unable to cross the intersection.

"Come on, girl," said Tanzan at once. Lifting her in his arms, he carried her over the mud. Ekido did not speak again until that night. When they reached a lodging temple, he no longer could restrain himself. "We monks are not supposed to go near women," he told Tanzan, "especially not young and lovely ones. It is dangerous. Why did you do that?"

"I left the girl there," said Tanzan. "Are you still carrying her?"

WHY DO YOU ENJOY
CHEWING ON OTHERS'
MISTAKES?

WHAT PLEASURE DO YOU
GET IN DOING SO?

HOW MUCH DO YOU
CHEW ON YOUR
OWN MISTAKES?

WISDOM

It was a quiet morning on Solomon's porch as a rapt crowd listened to the gentle words of Jesus. All of a sudden a woman was screaming, "No, no," as a group of well-dressed men dragged her through the crowd to where Jesus was sitting. Tears streaked her face, and she clutched her thin nightclothes to her bosom in terror and embarrassment.

Jesus stopped and waited. The spokesman from the group, an elderly Pharisee, flung a challenge at Jesus. "Teacher, this woman was caught in the very act of adultery. In the Law, Moses commanded us to stone such women. Now what do you say?" There was an uproar in the crowd.

Jesus glanced down and began writing on the dust covering the stones. The accusers shifted about and muttered to one another in impatience. Just then Jesus looked up to the old Pharisee and said, "The one of you who is without any sin, why don't you throw the first stone at her?" Then he leaned over and began doodling again.

The elderly Pharisee began to edge into the crowd and move away, trying not to attract attention. The younger men followed suit. All eyes followed their retreat till the echo of the last footfall died away.

Jesus looked up at the woman, conspicuous now, standing in front of the seated multitude. "Woman," he asked, "where are your accusers? Has no one passed sentence on you?"

"No one, Lord," she whispered.

"Then neither do I pass sentence on you," the Jesus said. "You can go now, but woman," he added, as she began to leave, "you must leave your life of sin." She nodded and walked back with the determination of a woman who had made up her mind.

39

WHAT ALL DO YOU
TAKE INTO
ACCOUNT WHEN
YOU ARE CALLED
UPON TO MAKE A
DECISION?

HOW WISE ARE
YOUR DECISIONS?

After I am gone

An old man went about planting mango saplings wherever he could. A young gardener was amused at the effort of the aging man and one day, unable to contain his curiosity, asked, "Sir, what gives you so much energy to plant these saplings, when you know that you may not even be there to see them flower or bear fruit?"

The old man replied, "These are for others to relish its fruits, just like I did all these years from trees which I have no idea who planted!"

40

WHAT IS IT THAT
YOU WOULD HAVE
LEFT BEHIND WHEN
YOU ARE GONE?

WHAT ARE YOU
BUSY PLANTING
IN YOUR
LIFE?

Set mind

A family of tortoises set out on a picnic. After some fun and frolic, when they unpacked the picnic basket, they realised there was no salt in the food.

It was decided the youngest would go and get some salt as he was the fastest. But the little one was worried that the others would eat all the food when he was away. After repeated assurances, the reluctant tortoise started.

They family waited for hours and hours, and then got so hungry that they decided to open the snacks and eat. That very moment, the little fellow jumped from a nearby bush and screamed, "Look, I knew you would not wait for me. All this time I was waiting behind the bushes to check on you. Now I am not going to get you any salt!"

The poisonous arrow

Was the man who shot me white or black?

Was he a native or a foreigner?

Was he tall or short?

A man was dying from a poisoned arrow. His relatives rushed a doctor to his side but he refused to have the arrow taken out unless he had the answers to three questions, very vital to him:

Was the man who shot him, white or black?

Was he a native or a foreigner?

Was he tall or short?

He was so adamant about getting his answers that the arrow could not be removed in time and he died.

WHAT ARE YOU BUSY WITH IN LIFE, THINGS THAT ARE TRIVIAL OR THOSE THAT ARE IMPORTANT?

HOW PRODUCTIVE ARE YOUR ENGAGEMENTS IN LIFE?

Convictions

The cook monk Dairyo, at Bankei's monastery, decided that he would take good care of his old teacher's health and give him only fresh miso, a paste of soy beans mixed with wheat and yeast that often ferments. Bankei, noticing that he was being served better miso than his pupils, asked: 'Who is the cook today?'

Dairyo was sent before him. Bankei learned that according to his age and position he should eat only fresh miso. So he said to the cook, "Then you think I shouldn't eat at all." With this he entered his room and locked the door. Dairyo, sitting outside the door, asked his teacher's pardon. Bankei would not answer.

43

For seven days Dairyo sat outside and Bankei within. Finally in desperation an adherent called loudly to Bankei, "You may be all right, old teacher, but this young disciple here has to eat. He cannot go without food forever!"

At this Bankei opened the door. He was smiling. He told Dairyo, "I insist on eating the same food as the rest of my followers. When you become a teacher I do not want you to forget this."

HOW STRONG ARE YOUR CONVICTIONS?

WHAT ARE YOU WILLING TO GIVE UP TO STAND BY YOUR CONVICTIONS?

44

Meet me halfway

After Nancy's business failed, she found herself in serious financial trouble. Desperately, she prayed to God to let her win the lotto so that she could save her house. But somebody else hit the jackpot on lotto night. This continued for some time and Nancy lost her house and car as well. Her children were starving. Again she desperately prayed that she should win the lotto. Suddenly, there was a bright flash in the sky. Nancy heard God's voice "Meet me halfway on this. Buy a lotto ticket."

DO YOU DO YOUR PART BEFORE YOU ASK OTHERS TO DO THEIRS, FOR WHAT YOU WISH FOR TO COME TRUE?

HOW DEPENDENT HAVE YOU BECOME IN YOUR LIFE?

Being Appropriate

45

A village temple was inhabited by an old snake, infamous for its nature to bite at the slightest pretext. The villagers were so full of fear that they were forced to abandon the place of worship. One day a sage, while passing through the village, started heading towards the temple. A villager rushed to him and warned him of the snake and its volatile temper. The sage said that he would take care of the snake and asked him to get the villagers to the temple. While at the temple he found the animal and offered to teach it a way out of its volatile temper by imparting a powerful *mantra*. The snake agreed to abide. He then spoke to the villagers on the need to keep the temple clean and perform the daily prayers. He assured them that the snake would not bother them any more and not to fear it.

On being assured by the sage, the villagers cleaned up the temple and started frequenting it like before. Now the snake had become so meek that children started pulling its tail, throwing stones at it and bruising it all over. Yet the snake adhered to its promise and remained calm.

Months passed. On another such visit, the sage was shocked to see the snake all bruised and wearier. "What happened?" he enquired. "All because of you!" complained the reptile. "True to your words, I have never harmed anyone, but see what they have done to me!" "Oh, you foolish animal!" chided the sage, "I had advised you not to bite anyone, but did I ever tell you not to hiss or raise your hood to protect yourself?"

DO YOU MOVE FROM ONE EXTREME TO THE OTHER OR DO YOU KNOW HOW TO BE IN A SPACE IN WHICH YOU ARE MOST APPROPRIATE?

HOW CONSCIOUS ARE YOU OF KNOWING WHEN TO BE WHAT?

Every minute counts!

The doctor's waiting room was crowded. An elderly gentleman who had been waiting for almost an hour, said to the receptionist, "I cannot wait any longer, would you kindly give me an appointment for another day?"

A woman seated next to him, whispered to her neighbour, "He must be at least eighty years old. What sort of urgent business does he have that he cannot afford to wait?" The old man who overheard the remark, said, "I am eighty-seven years old, lady, which is precisely why I cannot afford to waste a single minute of the precious time I am left with."

46

HOW MUCH TIME
ARE YOU LEFT
WITH TO DO WHAT
YOU WANT?

HOW OFTEN DO
YOU TAKE TIME
FOR GRANTED?

The Transformation

Grandma told us the most amazing stories of animals and birds. What made these stories unique was the wonderful message they had for our own lives.

The story of the Eagle, the magnificent king of the sky, struck me the most!

She would say, "Eagles enjoy a life of nearly seventy years. But this gift of a long life has not been bestowed upon them; it is a choice they have to make!"

"When they touch nearly forty years of their life, their beaks have grown old and curved, their claws are hardened and their feathers are heavy and bulky. If they continue with these, they cannot catch their prey and will soon die. But if they want to extend their life, they have to make a choice, a choice of undergoing a painful transformation, a transformation that will make them live for another thirty years or more."

47

"They have to fly to the top of a mountain and make it their home for the next five months. These months are the most painful when they have to hit their beaks against the hard rocks till they fall and a new one appears. With their new beak, they pull out their old nails and wait for new ones to grow. The new nails help them weed out their old feathers. With this renewed strength, they get to live again!"

ARE YOU HAPPY LIVING WHAT YOU HAVE ALREADY BECOME OR DO YOU WANT TO TRANSFORM YOURSELF?

ARE YOU WILLING TO PUT IN THE EFFORT IT TAKES TO TRANSFORM YOURSELF?

What I don't take is not mine

Buddha and his disciple were moving from house to house begging for alms. The lady of one of the houses, before coming to the door, let out a stream of abuse. *Buddha* moved on and the hurt disciple followed him. Surprised to find him unperturbed by the incident, he asked the master how he could remain unaffected by her behaviour. At this point, *Buddha* asked him to turn around and look at the house. The lady, bound by tradition, had now come to the door to offer alms but finding no one at the door, took it back in.

Buddha then told his disciple, "What I don't take is not mine."

48

HOW EASILY DO YOU
ALLOW YOURSELF TO BE
IMPACTED BY ALL THAT
HAPPENS AROUND YOU?

WHAT HOLDS YOU FROM
MAKING A CHOICE OF
WHAT WILL AFFECT YOU
AND WHAT WILL NOT?

Caring

A stag and a doe were lost in a desert, thirsty and tired. On the verge of collapsing, they spotted a tiny oasis glittering in the sun. They reached out in hope, just to find a mouthful of water. The stag put his mouth forward, pretended to take a sip and let his mate quench her thirst after him.

Very soon the stag lost his life, but at peace as it was for the one he truly loved!

49

WHAT IS THE EXTENT
TO WHICH YOU CARE?
DOES YOUR CARE GO
BEYOND YOUR OWN
SELF?

CHINESE BAMBOO

A young student once told his master, "I have been working very hard for a very long time but I have not got any results till now. I am very disheartened". On hearing this, the master smiled and said, "You plant a Chinese bamboo and water it, nurture it, tend it, nothing happens for five years! And just when you start to give up, in the next six weeks, it grows to a height of ninety feet!"

The student understood what the master was trying to say and never complained again.

DO YOU REALISE THAT YOUR FOUNDATION FOR GROWTH TAKES A LOT MORE TIME AND EFFORT THAN GROWTH ITSELF?

HOW STRONG IS YOUR FOUNDATION?

ARE YOU LETTING IMPATIENCE COME IN THE WAY OF YOUR GROWTH?

It's in your hands...

A learned old man was highly respected by the simple village folks for his wisdom and timely counsel. All but one cynical young man, who wanted to outwit him in front of the villagers...

Here's a trick to prove the old man wrong! I will ask him to predict if this little bird in my hand is dead or alive...If he says it's dead, I will set it free and if he says, it's alive , I will crush it to death...

"Oh, learned one! Can you tell me if the little bird in my hand is alive or dead?"

51

The wise man saw through the youngster's trick and replied...

"Son, the answer lies entirely in your hands!"

HOW WISE ARE YOU TO TEST OTHERS' WISDOM?

DO YOU REALISE THAT WISDOM IS SUPERIOR TO INTELLIGENCE?

The Sculptor

A tourist saw a sculptor busy sculpting an idol of a deity, near a temple under construction. He noticed a similar idol lying nearby. He asked curiously, "Do you need two similar idols?"

"No," said the sculptor without looking up, "we need only one, but the first one got damaged in the final stages."

The tourist examined the idol and found no apparent damage. "Where is the damage?" he asked. "There is a scratch on the nose of the idol," said the sculptor, still busy with his work.

"Where are you going to install the idol?" enquired the onlooker. "On a pillar twenty feet high," came the reply. "At such a distance," exclaimed the tourist, "who would ever know that there is a scratch?"

The sculptor stopped his work, looked up at the tourist, smiled and said, "I will!"

52

WHAT IS YOUR OWN
STANDARD OF QUALITY
IN ALL THAT YOU DO?

WHAT MAKES YOU
COMPROMISE?

CUT THE ROPE

Once a mountain climber, determined to reach the summit of a high mountain, prepared relentlessly for years and began his adventure. He began the ascent all alone as he wanted all the glory to himself. He continued climbing even as daylight faded, night fell and there was total darkness around. But he wouldn't stop.

He was just a few meters away from the summit when to his horror, he slipped on a ridge and started falling at frightening speed. All he could feel was an inexplicable panic and the tug of gravity sucking him into nothingness. In those moments of anguish he saw his entire life pass before his eyes and was almost giving up, when he felt the rope tighten around his waist.

In desperation, suspended in mid-air he screamed, "God, please help me!"

Suddenly a deep voice resounded from the heavens above, "What do you want me to do?"

"Please save me!"

"Do you really think I can save you?'

"Of course, my Lord!"

"Well then, cut the rope."

There was a moment of silence. Then the man tightened the rope further around his waist.

Two days later, the mountain rescue team found a man frozen to death, his hands wrapped firmly around a rope tied to his waist…two feet away from the ground!

53

WRAPPED IN THE
IGNORANCE OF YOUR
KNOWLEDGE, HOW OFTEN
DO YOU IGNORE THE
WISDOM COMING FROM
CONSCIOUSNESS?

HOW MUCH DO YOU
UNDERSTAND AND USE
THE HELP THAT COMES
TO YOU?

The New Robe

A disciple came to *Buddha* and complained, "Master, my attire is worn out and it is beyond decency to wear the same."

Buddha found the robe indeed in a bad condition and asked the store keeper to give him a new one. The disciple thanked them and retired to his room.

A few days later, *Buddha* went to the disciple's humble abode and asked, "Is your new attire comfortable? Do you need anything else?"

"Thank you Master. The attire is indeed comfortable. I need nothing more."

54

"Having got the new one, what did you do with your old attire?"

"I am using it as my bed spread."

"Then...hope you have disposed off your old bed spread?"

"No, no master. It is being used as my window curtain."

"And what about your old curtain?"

"That is used to handle the hot utensils in the kitchen."

"Oh! I see. Can you tell me what they did with the old cloth in the kitchen?"

"It is being used to wash the floor."

"And the old rug being used to wash the floor?"

"Master, since it was torn off so much, we could not find any better use, but to use it as a wick in the oil lamp, which is right now lit in your study room."

Buddha smiled in contentment and left.

WHAT DOES IT TAKE FOR ONE'S LIFE TO BE COMPLETELY UTILIZED?

WHAT IS THE PURPOSE OF ONE'S EXISTENCE?

How much land does a man need?

An emperor once challenged his horseman to ride his horse across as much ground as he could. He promised to give him an equivalent of the area covered.

The horseman rose to the challenge and rode his horse as fast as he could. In his greed, he beat his horse to ride faster and did not bother to stop for food or rest.

The horseman covered a very substantial area, but was close to exhaustion and death. In his final moments he realised that all the land covered was of no use...finally all that he needed was a small plot for his grave.

Who is watching?

Kanakadasa was in his *gurukul* with his friends, when the teacher came in with a bunch of ripe bananas. He asked each student to take one and eat it in a place where no one could see them. Each ran and hid in different places and feasted on the fruit. Only Kanakadasa kept sitting with the fruit in hand. A few of his friends mocked at him for not succeeding in such a simple task.

When asked by the teacher, he replied, "There is no place where no one is watching me! Where ever I go, I can still see myself!"

WHAT STOPS YOU FROM WATCHING YOURSELF?

HOW IGNORANT ARE YOU ABOUT YOUR OWN SELF?

WHERE IS YOUR CONSCIENCE?

DANDELIONS

A man took great pride in his lawn. Once, on his return from a trip abroad, he found a large crop of dandelions in his lawn. He tried every method he knew to destroy them. Still they plagued him. Finally he wrote to the Department of Agriculture. He enumerated all the things he had tried, and closed the letter with the question: "What shall I do now?"

In due course the reply came: "We suggest you learn to love them."

57

HOW OFTEN DO YOU REALISE THAT ACCEPTING YOUR LIMITATIONS IS THE FIRST STEP IN DEALING WITH THEM?

What next?

A successful businessman dealing in furniture returned from a journey to find his shop and house burnt, along with all his property.

His only action was putting up a signboard on the scene of the shambles:

Shop burnt
House burnt
goods burnt
But faith not burnt
starting business tomorrow

HOW STRONG ARE YOU?
WHAT IS YOUR THRESHOLD?
WHAT IN YOU MAKES YOU
GIVE UP?

The Crossroads

Once a young man was loitering around and reached a particular crossroad, which led in many different directions. He was confused as to which led where, and spotting an elderly person near by, enquired...

THE ONE I FEED

A native American boy was talking to his grandfather. "What do you think about the world situation?" he asked.

The grandfather replied, "I feel like two wolves are fighting in my heart. One full of anger and hatred. The other full of love, forgiveness and peace."

"Which one will win?", asked the boy.

To which the grandfather replied, "The one I feed."

HOW CONSCIOUS ARE
YOU OF WHAT YOU ARE
FEEDING WITHIN YOU?

HOW MUCH CONTROL
DO YOU HAVE ON WHO
YOU FEED?

ST★R FISH

A man saw a human figure at a distance on the beach, who seemed to be dancing with the waves. As he approached, he realised it was a young boy picking up starfish from the shores of the beach and throwing them into the breaking waves in a graceful pattern.

"What are you doing?" he asked in amusement.

The boy stopped what he was doing and replied, "The sun is up and the waves are receding. I am sending these starfish back to where they came from!"

"But the shore stretches for miles and miles together and there are thousands of starfish all over! Do you think you will ever make a difference?"

The boy smiled, bent down, picked up a starfish, threw it into the breaking waves with the same graceful movement and said, "It made a difference to that one!"

The man went back deep in thought, came back the next morning and joined the boy in throwing the starfish into the mighty sea!

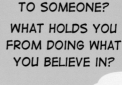

DO YOU REALISE THAT EVERY SMALL DEED OF YOURS CAN MAKE A DIFFERENCE TO SOMEONE?

WHAT HOLDS YOU FROM DOING WHAT YOU BELIEVE IN?

The Little Girl
who came with an umbrella

"Ah! There has been no rain for almost an year now!"

"How are we to feed our families?"

"It is a curse on us…we need to appease the gods!"

The gathering near the village banyan tree was a spectacle of distress. The village headman was thrown in deep concern as he contemplated a way out of the severe drought the village was facing.

After much thought, he announced, "Let the entire village start preparing for the grand service to the rain god, two days from now. I am sure the plea of a thousand hearts would not go unheard!"

The news was spread and the convinced villagers started preparing for the grand service. On the auspicious day, the entire village assembled at the place where the worship was to take place.

But only one little girl came with an umbrella!

WHAT IS
THE LEVEL OF FAITH
YOU HAVE IN THE MANY
THINGS YOU DO?

IS YOUR DOUBT (CONSCIOUS OR
UNCONSCIOUS), A CAUSE FOR
YOUR OWN FAILURE?

Salt Doll

A salt doll journeyed for thousands of miles and stopped on the edge of the sea. It was fascinated by this moving liquid mass, so unlike anything it had seen before. "What are you?" the salt doll asked the sea.

"Come in and see!" invited the sea with a smile.

So the doll walked in. The further it went the more it dissolved till there was only a pinch of salt left.

Before that last bit dissolved, the doll exclaimed in wonder, "Now I know what I am!"

DO YOU REALISE THAT WHEN YOU COMPLETELY IMMERSE YOURSELF IN ANYTHING, YOU END UP DISCOVERING YOURSELF?

WHAT HOLDS YOU FROM UNDERSTANDING THAT EVERYTHING IS A PART OF YOU AND YOU ARE A PART OF EVERYTHING?

One Step
at a Time

64

A farmer found a little boy sobbing away in darkness, holding a tiny oil lamp by his side.

"What's the matter?" asked the farmer.

The boy lifted his tear stricken face and said, "I need to cross the forest to reach my village on the other side. My mother is waiting for me. But I am so scared of the dark."

"But you have a lamp with you." the farmer suggested.

"Yes I do, but it can show me only a few feet of the way and the village is at least three miles away!" complained the boy amidst sobs.

The wise farmer made the boy stand up and asked him to take a step, "Just watch one step at a time as shown by the lamp and you will reach home!"

The boy took every step in light and soon reached his village without fear.

WHERE DO YOUR FEARS STEM FROM?

HOW OFTEN DO YOUR FEARS BLIND YOU FROM SEEING THE VALUE OF ALL THAT YOU HAVE?

"There is a beginning and an end

in every step I take.

There is a continuous movement

in all my steps.

The beginnings and ends are a part of

the larger beginning and end.

I have just started,

I am sure one day I will reach."

J M Sampath

As you travel in your own journey, do take some time and share your reflections with us. We would appreciate your views on this book.
Write to us at **feedback@insightpublishers.com**

Other publications by the same author

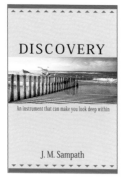

Discovery is a transformative learning tool that aims to introduce basic human values to a person and initiate a process of self-enquiry. It is a first of its kind methodology employed by people worldwide, in organizations or as individuals, as a tool to aid them look deep within. The first edition was printed in 1989 and has subsequently undergone three reprints and translation into other languages, following an encouraging response from a wide cross-section of readers.

Inner Realities is an interesting collection of personal notes, quotes and poems, drawn from the author's personal observations and experiences of life. It is filled with profound wisdom on personal growth and values. It aspires to aid people to live with awareness and lead a rich life out of understanding. A simple yet effective narrative style makes it easier to relate with. Having undergone two reprints, this little book is a true companion for life.

Insight Publishers is a young publishing company with a clear vision to enhance the level of consciousness in the larger social system. With a strong humane foundation, our essence of being is to nurture wisdom and we are keen to tread and explore any path, both known and unknown, towards the realisation of this aspiration of ours.

Our aim is to bring out books and artefacts that will aid us in our quest for maturing into fine individuals. Our work in this space is motivated by a vision of nurturing wisdom through partnering with fellow students of life. We have faith in the inner power to affect positive changes in our lives and welcome you to undertake this journey with us, in the path of self-actualisation.

www.insightpublishers.com